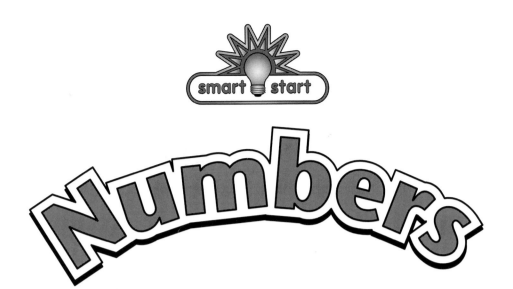

Numbers

Please visit our web site at: www.garethstevens.com
For a free color catalog describing Gareth Stevens' list of high-quality books and
multimedia programs, call 1-800-542-2595 (USA) or 1-800-461-9120 (Canada).
Gareth Stevens Publishing's Fax: (414) 332-3567.

Library of Congress Cataloging-in-Publication Data available upon request from publisher.
Fax (414) 336-0157 for the attention of the Publishing Records Department.

ISBN 0-8368-2845-3

This edition first published in 2001 by
Gareth Stevens Publishing
A World Almanac Education Group Company
330 West Olive Street, Suite 100
Milwaukee, WI 53212 USA

Design concept: Derome Design, Inc.
English translation: Patricia Lantier
English text: Dorothy L. Gibbs and Heidi Sjostrom
Cover design: Scott Krall

Printed in the United States of America

1 2 3 4 5 6 7 8 9 05 04 03 02 01

smart start

Numbers

Roger Paré

Gareth Stevens Publishing
A WORLD ALMANAC EDUCATION GROUP COMPANY
28 AVERY ROW
ROANOKE, VIRGINIA 24012-8828

This colorful clown has only **one** hair to put under his hat.

Two big rhinos are much too heavy for one small bicycle!

My birthday cake has **three** candles. Guess how old I am.

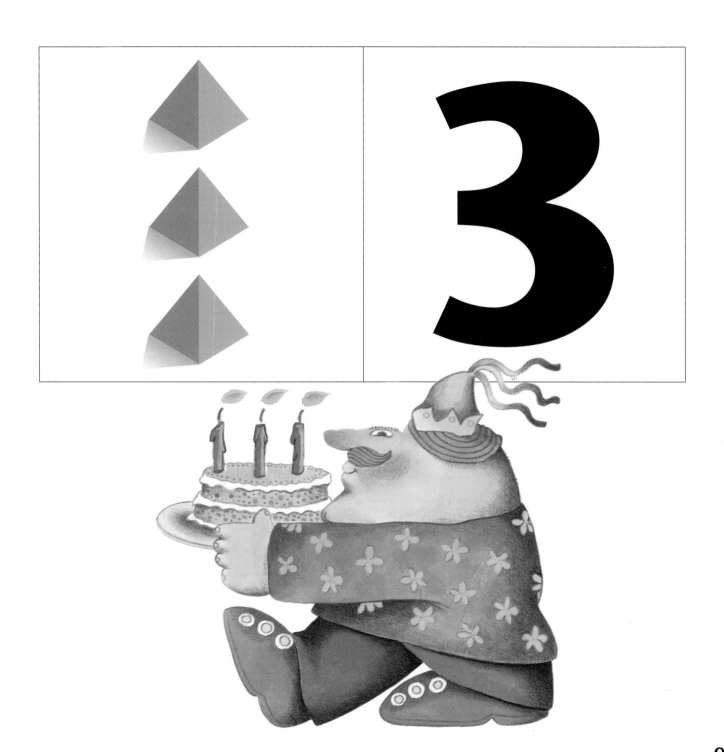

3

9

Four lively cats have a friendly
fight before they fall asleep.

4

Larry LaRue has lost his shoe.
His **five** fat toes are freezing!

5

This musical monkey can play **six** notes on the saxophone.

6

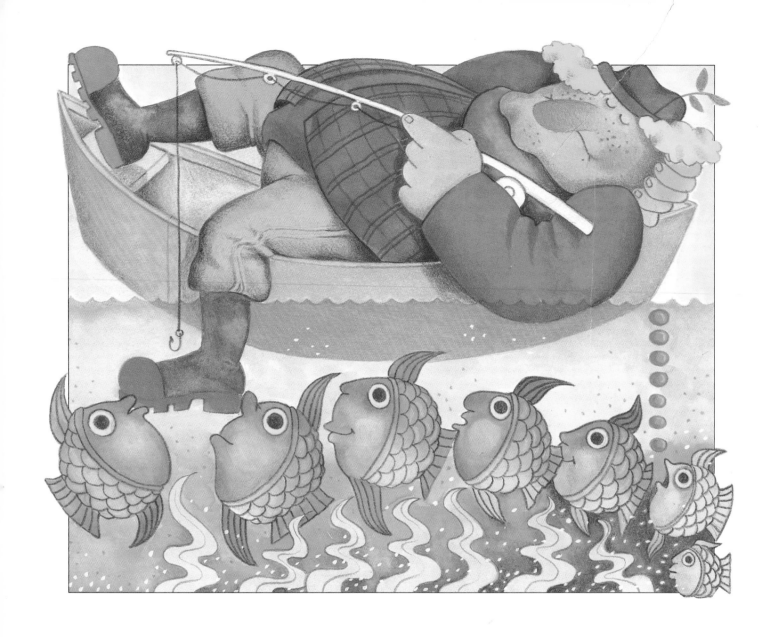

Seven fish spy a boat and a boot. Watch out for that hook!

7

Eight red flowers need lots of showers to help them grow.

Nine suitcases are stacked on the train for a trip to Maine.

9

Ten ripe, red apples will
make a tart and tasty treat.

10

More Books on Numbers

Counting. *Mortimer's Math* (series). Karen Bryant-Mole (Gareth Stevens)

Dreaming: A Countdown to Sleep. Elaine Greenstein (Arthur A. Levine)

Numbers. *Little Mouse's Learn-and-Play* (series). Anaël Dena (Gareth Stevens)

One Duck Stuck. Phyllis Root and Jane Chapman (Candlewick Press)

One Lonely Sea Horse. Saxton Freymann and Joost Elffers (Arthur A. Levine)

Ten Black Dots. Donald Crews (Econo-Clad Books)

 # Web Sites

Get Counting.
www.familychannel.ca/f_stuff/games/countinggame/counting_game.html

Hidden Number.
www.etch-a-sketch.com/html/find123.htm